CENTRAL ENGLAND 1999

Edited by

Andrew Head

First published in Great Britain in 1999 by
POETRY NOW
1-2 Wainman Road, Woodston,
Peterborough, PE2 7BU
Telephone (01733) 230746
Fax (01733) 230751

HB ISBN 0 75430 566 X
SB ISBN 0 74530 567 8

FOREWORD

Although we are a nation of poetry writers we are accused of not reading poetry and not buying poetry books: after many years of listening to the incessant gripes of poetry publishers, I can only assume that the books they publish, in general, are books that most people do not want to read.

Poetry should not be obscure, introverted, and as cryptic as a crossword puzzle: it is the poet's duty to reach out and embrace the world.

The world owes the poet nothing and we should not be expected to dig and delve into a rambling discourse searching for some inner meaning.

The reason we write poetry (and almost all of us do) is because we want to communicate: an ideal; an idea; or a specific feeling.

Poetry is as essential in communication, as a letter; a radio; a telephone, and the main criteria for selecting the poems in this anthology is very simple: they communicate.

CONTENTS

No Respect

There are times when I feel alone,
but this is what I've come to expect.
Not often do people use the phone,
to offer the love and respect.
At times when I'm feeling really low,
and all I need is love.
I feel the need to let people know,
that I'm not someone that they can shove.
I feel my life has always been affected,
by the mindless, thoughtless ways,
of people who have never respected,
ever, throughout their days.
In order to gain respect from me,
is to give it in return.
I hope one day these people will see,
that their lack of respect causes concern.

Michaela Garlick

TOGETHER APART

Once it was sad to take our leave
Where only stairs caused separation
Until morning called
And friendship was renewed
Another day.

Now valley, river
Field and hill
Mark out the miles
While winding road
Both separates and joins
The lives once shared
Behind one door.

Each twist and turn
A landmark,
While each remembered church
Each farm, each resting place along the way
Allows a journey in the mind
Which soothes the pain
Of living far apart.

Yet separation of the heart
Seems no more real
Than when one roof was shared.

Each moment finds some thought
Tracing its way across the mind.
Rich memories of childhood joys
Join hands with future hope
As heartache, never far away
Is moved from centre stage
Into the corner of our lives.

Charles Rice

THE BARN OWL

'Tis dusk at the barn - and the shadows are long,
Laden cows are being milked in the dairy shed.
A solitary blackbird trills his evensong -
And the weary farmer longs for his bed.

The rounded pigs snore in the sty
And the striped farm cat curls up in the hay.
A flock of geese fly across the crimson sky
In salute to the fading day.

A badger forages in the sorrel leaves
And fluttering moths replace the butterflies in flight.
Sleepy swallows rest in the stable eaves
Whilst bats in the rafters anticipate the night.

The barn now becomes an eerie place -
The light is almost no more.
Overlooked by a ghostly face,
The mice gather on the corn covered floor.

They do not see his steely glare -
Or hear phantom wings pursue their prey
As he gracefully glides through the air,
'Tis the barn owl's time of day!

The clock in the village strikes eight
And the startled mice scatter in the straw
Alas for one poor mouse - it is too late
But that is nature's law.

Lorraine Marler

BY STATHERN BRIDGE

Across the cornfields,
Image sharp, hedges and trees
3-d'd by bright sun
Give landscapes fresh reality.

As if paint spattered,
Single columbine flowers
Polka - white on green -
Along the canal reed beds.

Sun-roused dragonflies
Quarter and skim the canal.
Helicoptering.
Jerking left, then right, stop, start.

Amongst the hawthorns
Early August blackberries
Beats the autumn hedgers,
Treats towpath bramblers.

Humping the canal
The bridge blocks a driver's view.
His hooted warning
Is alien to the scene.

On this, Stathern Bridge,
I saw my first free snake wind,
And tragedy strike
As a swan flew into wires.

Once, north of the Bridge,
Shrub sheltered, white violets grew.
No more. Dogs pay calls
To this council cleared spot now.

You think that it takes housing estates to destroy
Nature's paradise?
It takes a lot less than that.

R L Cooper

FOR THE LATE GREAT MARC BOLAN

(Marc Bolan - 20th Century Boy (30 September 1947-16 September 1977) - Sadly missed - Never forgotten)

I cannot believe, that it has been twenty years,
As from my eyes, I wipe away the tears,
As I think of you, and how your life was so cruelly taken,
Each year, the pain in my heart it awakens.

I remember well, that day in nineteen seventy seven,
When Marc Bolan was taken from us, to his place in heaven,
I heard the news that day, and not one word I wanted to believe,
As for you, I never ever wanted to grieve.

You gave us so much, so much pleasure, so much joy,
I grew up with your music, from when I was a boy,
It saw me through the good times, and through bad,
And it was the only comfort, that I ever had.

Despite all the sadness, your life was not in vain,
As your music still thrills us, and will always remain,
Forever in our hearts, in our souls, and in our minds,
So thank you Marc Bolan, you will be remembered for all time.

Philip S Robinson

GRASMERE

I look to your
Snowy mountain tops,
Down to you
Sweet waters below,
How serene you look,
I wonder how
Many awed feet
Have trampled upon
Your rocky footpaths,
I often think of
When your valley
Was first formed
All those long
Glacier years ago,
I often ponder on
How you looked
Before modern man
Discovered you and
Trampled on you.
Oh, how I look
Upon you with
Such awe and passion,
Whilst you stare
Aloft to heaven
With all your proud might,
Shining forth God's
Power and love to all.

Penny Wright

BLACK HILL - SUMMER 1996

Black mud, thick like treacle, grips at my boots
I look down. Rain-soaked sponge gives out under my weight
Where hard flagged path had supported me.

Death Clough behind me, Black Dike Head above
Excitement gives way to aching thighs and a cold sweat -
Though it is still one walk amongst many.

Turns out Black Dike Head is no summit, its cairn only a half-way
marker
Each contributory stone symbolic of a thousand frustrated climbs -
The prospect of Black Hill becomes daunting.

Trig point. Where is it? The top; it should be visible
I have not come all this way to climb half a mountain -
Two thousand feet. Advancing mist. I quicken the pace.

Endless black peat dunes moated by wind-rippled rainwater
My legs wet to the knees. I run. I, I begin to panic -
Amidst the search, I am becoming disorientated.

This barren desert plateau shows some pity. The trig point
It is there ahead, only I can't get to it, a maze of dunes
And pools to negotiate.

Black Hill. All I've ever thought it was and yet more sinister.
Sinister in afternoon sunlight with clear blue sky. How would it be
In the blackest, bleakest winter weather?

Black is the description. A square mile in the sky where nothing takes
root.
I pause at the top for barely a minute, then descend with a pace -
And I find myself looking back with intrigue, over and over.

Simon Collison

RHYTHM OF LIFE

Do you see poetry
With eyes that are blind
Do the words and the prose
Form pictures in your mind

Do you hear poetry
With ears that are deaf
Do the words and the prose
Sound warm on your breath

Do you speak poetry
When you can't make a sound
Do the words and the prose
Shout to you aloud

Do you feel poetry
When emotionally drained
Do the words and the prose
Lift spirits, restrained

You are the poetry
Your verse is your own
Expression is freedom
Not senses alone.

Jacquelyn Harby

THE WAY OF LIFE

Life goes rushing headlong by -
The days and months just seem to fly -
There's barely time to stop and gaze,
At nature's beautiful displays -
Or to refresh our spirits in life's rush,
Which the eternal treadmill seems to crush;
But amid life's never-ending pace,
We all need time to halt the race -
To renew our spiritual desires -
And all to which our soul aspires.

Angela E Setford

THE ART OF WORDS

There is no Art
Without the Words
Without the Poet
Who describes it.

Communicating each intimate detail
Art's static form hides a certain beauty
With so many given words
To describe what is best seen.

As Art informs us
Of what is seen
Words can only interpret
The truth in its scene.

By the Words we use
And the Art we choose
We can hear such beauty
That sight has in store.

No explanation given
Of worthy intent
Allows such explanation
Without a word's lament.

What compliments the chosen word
In that scene it beholds
Of the Artist's impression
As his vision unfolds.

Patrick Dempsey

SECRET WISH

False becoming smiles put on for all,
But the childlike tears, too eagerly fall.

Conquering battles, loneliness and despair,
A broken lost soul, takes love from anywhere.

Another day, and a new dawn of hope,
So you convince yourself again today, you'll cope.

Repetitive days and pillow hugging at night,
Realisation, you've returned to this circle of life.

Constantly pushing, and striving to survive,
You eventually scream, 'Am I meant to be alive!'

Such simple plain words, can easily show,
How bitter torments from life, can make you grow.

But the beautiful smile, will always continue,
And the secret wish, that the tears will dwindle.

R Williams

CONTEMPLATION

If only I had heard the phone call
The music was just too loud
If only I had heard the key in the door
Warning Mum and Dad had arrived
If only the word hadn't been passed around by all
'The party's at number two.'
If only the refreshments hadn't been spilt on the floor
The house is just too small
If only it hadn't been called a party
Just a small gathering of friends
If only the word 'sorry' would remove the stains in the carpet
The ruling of bedroom confinement would end.

Victoria A Bodycote

FOR HIM, WITHIN THE SHADOWS . . .

Sweet friend of mine, I thank you and I know it's not enough,
For the times that you are with me when the going becomes rough,
For the ways in which you come to me and hold me safe and well,
For the comfort that you give me when the pain begins to swell.

I felt until I met you that I never would belong,
The colours are too harsh for me, and people are too strong
So I cannot fight against them, but my heart's not made of stone.
Some people are not meant to be cast out in life alone.

I couldn't look you in the eye that day when we first met.
You understood that to me all humanity's a threat.
You knew without me saying so my heart was made of dust,
That the nightmares stole my dreams away and I had no need of trust.

I tear myself apart with all the pain I hold inside
And never thought to live again when the love within me died.
But you challenge me to face it. So I try to stand up tall
And fight against my nature, and you catch me when I fall.

You hold my hand, you nuzzle, you lead me to my fear
With every faltering step I take I sense that you are near
And when I back away from it you're always there to scold me
But if I crash back down to earth you seek me out and hold me.

You watch me from the shadows, smiling amusement at my woe,
Stepping from them briefly, just to wink and let me know
That you are there beside me and you promise you will stay,
And that love and trust do exist and are not just games we play.

Jeannie Sharp

WET, WET, WET 1998

February fill dike black or white
Why didn't it happen?
Did Mother Nature forget?
We sat in the sunshine and saw the daffodils
Beware - it's not too late even yet.

April's here and so is the rain
White weddings are planned
So Good Friday received a carpet of snow
Too much to hold in store
Too much to cope with so floods galore.

May gave us a taste of summer
So good to feel the sun
We thought it was here to stay
It wasn't long before it went away
June and July back to rain and wet, wet, wet!

Myrtle E Holmes

LOVE OF A LADY

The taste of summer dew,
The look of winter morn,
The moon that gleams your shine,
The sun that does adorn.
Your eyes that sparkle like stars
The breeze of spring in your step,
Your voice of warmth that eases the pain,
Which yesterday begun.
The rose, its thorns
Its flourishing colour
The passionate wind, flapping petals to the ground,
The stillness of beauty in which the flower blooms
Is all that keeps you in your mysterious shroud.

W Wright

THE PHOENIX DEATH

In this last week trees are just lit and smoulder
Burning up the year in their timely fires,
Fogged and banked to softened hues of sunset
As the year sinks towards winter's silent oath,
In this once mild and generous clime.

The golden garden glows with dying leaves,
The 'suckle's scarlet droop and that last, perfect rose
Before rot sets its myriad striving buds to smoky fur;
'Anne's lustrous cups climbing as she turns to flame
Through boughs of misted leaves loved by bees and I for's scented
blue;
Knautia, neat splashed knots of purpled Grecian blood;
The hare's last violet bells, shivering round its froth of dead
As few flax candle tips light grey days for bees.

Yet midst all this final flaunt there's new felicity,
Waterlily's lilac pom-poms fountain from the quiet earth;
The first magenta movement in the clematis' high swung spray;
The hope of crocus; arum's rosy noses snouting through the soil
Scenting spring, as rosed orbs hang, waxing fat
Amid the diademed and the grass's ghosting young.

Sue Pierce

FAREWELL TO SUMMER

Swallows,
Sitting in a line on the telegraph wires.
Gossiping.
Gathering in ever increasing numbers.
Darting to and fro,
Discussing their journey
Or the summer they have had.
How do they know when to go;
What tells them?
Is it the frosty nights;
Dew on the grass?
Twittering,
Tirelessly.
Swooping,
Suddenly,
They've flown.
Farewell to summer.

Tessa A Meetham

NIL DESPERANDUM - (DESPAIR OF NOTHING)

My thoughts lie troubled, anxious fears
That plague my soul, my mind in tears
Contemplating the coming years
Resolved I hope soon to revere
A better life, adventing cheer.

Nature's reveries befits my dreams
I try to lift my hopes, my schemes
To blow away the dismal means,
Again to capture hope redeemed,
Be lifted back within life's theme.

Victim of mine own despair
I clamber, straining to highest stair
Run the gauntlet of this I dare
Seeing light afar, finding I really care
To take up the gift of life and love and willing to share.

Dorothy Athorn

Awaken The Memory

In a coffin buried deep underground
There lies a story eternally bound
Weeds choke the words in stone
While he and his thoughts fade away to bone

Maggots are squirming in the dark
Eating away the soul of his heart
A fire burns in the graveyard cold
Destroying all that he ever told

No one goes to visit him
We're all too busy with lives of sin
Remember the place he had in your mind
Engrave it so it's easy to find

Claire Hunnisett

HAVOC

Not a steady person
A little paranoid
Of judgements made by others
About my tear stained soul
Rebellious before
Not silent even now
I lost my mind
Saw it slip away
Across the shiny floor
Even sat and watched it
A streak of evil
Flashes through inside
In red hot days
I'll try standing
Bathed in shining light
Idle in recrimination
Time may not see me
Inside the feelings it's
Best to keep a smile
For special occasions
I'm going to cause havoc
In the cold evening quiet
Of all your lives.

Alison Crawford-Ward

THE WAITING DEW

In the shadow of a valley lies the early morning dew,
Hiding from sunlight just peeping through,
A breeze caressing a clear blue sky,
Silently watching the world go by,
Sounds hover, then disappear,
Before reaching the horizon never near,
Whispers brush the listening minds,
Or float through hanging vines,
Sleep lingers then is gone,
But not away from everyone,
The sun stalks the waiting dew,
Warming the earth patient and true,
As the colours that blend and are there,
Constant with the morning air,
That is invisible yet free to roam,
Choosing a resting place or home,
Perhaps noticing the dew cannot move or run,
Away from the devouring sun.

G Bateson

UNTITLED

Soft teardrops fall and wet my cheek.
They voice the words I cannot speak.
The thousand words that fill my head
Now that my loved one is dead.

Each one portrays the grief I feel -
The grief I won't admit is real.
It hurts so bad, it cuts so deep,
It taints my dreams - I cannot sleep.

For though I know your soul lives on,
And to a new life you have gone,
I want you here with me, today.
I want you here with me - to stay.

Don't you know my heart is breaking?
Don't you know my soul's been aching?
Every minute, every day,
Ever since you went away.

Your absence only feeds my love.
Your absence sows the seeds, my love.
The seeds which one day I shall reap
When I, too, find eternal sleep.

Then I shall join you once again,
And put an end to all this pain.

Anita M Kilbourne

Logic's Confusion

What makes people do what they do?
What makes them think that it is alright to hurt and kill?
The end does not justify the means, it never has.

Is this all that you know? Is this all your twisted souls can see?
A voice louder than yours has been heard, it's time for you to listen
There is no point putting your hands over your ears.
It's time for the killing to stop.

Look at your people, look at your children.
Look deep into their eyes and tell me what you see.
What point to civil war when it's your children that you hurt?
What point to terrorism when it's your people that suffer?
It's time to move on, time to compromise for all our sakes.

There is enough pain in the world without you adding to it,
There is no point claiming land when there is no one to live upon it.
No point persecuting those that have a different religion.
Have two world wars taught us nothing?
Have all those people died for nothing?

It's time to look around at what your single-mindedness has got you.
Time to count the cost, to look deeper at what makes you do these
                                                    things.
It isn't for religion, it isn't for family, or for country.
It's murder, it's all you know, it's what you have become.
Forget fear, forget anger, it's time for the killing to stop.

Julie Rickett

A Grandmother's Outing

The sun was shining up on high,
It was a lovely day.
We all assembled at the car,
And we were on our way.

The traffic was a great surprise
We hardly moved at all.
The weather started closing in,
And rain began to fall.

The children started, 'How long now?'
I wondered that myself,
When there, at last, the cottage stood
Upon a rocky shelf.

A good night's sleep had changed our mood.
With picnic packed in time.
In heavy boots, and well wrapped up
We started off to climb.

The others, all had reached the top,
'Come on! Come on!' they cried.
They waved their hands, and beckoned as
With dragging steps I tried.

A passing climber, walking down,
Stopped as he saw my plight.
Said, 'To the RSPCG's
Now I shall surely write.

Indignantly, I carried on,
And shortly reached the top.
In triumph I surveyed the view
Next time - at home I'll stop.

Mair Alexander

I COULDN'T HELP NOTICE

I saw you with your new man last night
and couldn't help notice the way the light
that shone so brightly upon your face
lit up the shadows but revealed no trace
of the frowns you showed to me.

And as you left you smiled and waved
and I couldn't help notice the look you gave
your lover as he kissed your hand,
and you spread your fingers wide and fanned
his cheek, like you never did to me.

And after you'd gone I sat with my drink
and couldn't help notice the way I think
about you - endlessly.

Which is very strange
as I was doing ok
And hadn't noticed I loved you - anyway.

Lynn Senior

EMBRACE THE DAY

Darkness covers the land like a veil covers a face,
a moment in your life disappears without trace.
Who will remember when you have gone,
will it be your daughter will it be your son then again maybe
it will be none.
We leave behind memories and things we have done,
disappointments and joys adventures nearly begun.
All our pain it counts for nothing all those lonely hours,
thoughts flow down the grates of time in showers.
All the people we have known, the times shared meaningless.
The anger and frustration in your life it is here I confess.
Live your life and use it as you will never stop living until
you are still.
For when you are no more what is to say you ever were here.
An act of bravery a noble deed or perhaps the love you gave
someone, yes, the latter I think indeed.
Life is but lent to us of this I am sure, each one is different
like the waves upon a shore.
I wonder how many people through time have written such words as
these yet forgotten as I am sure I will be.
How many eyes have gazed upon the moon at night inspired to do
so by love despair or fright.
But once I am gone what will be said, who will be left behind
And will their hearts be dead.
Of the past I am content, of the future I am unsure, of the
present let us embrace each day, embrace each day.

Dean Marc Brailsford

FLOATING

Floating, on the crest of a wave
The ripples of the water brush against me
They caress my skin, my arms, my feet
They send a shudder through my thoughts, my soul, my being,
So high, so fast.
Its very energy holds me, pushes me, and sweeps me
From this reality to another.

Floating, on the crest of a wave
Before I am pulled deep
Deep into unconsciousness
Where the warmth surrounds my body,
The silence surrounds my mind.
Everything is new
It is safe beneath the waves.

Floating, on the crest of a wave
Where can I be? What can I be? Who can I be?
This impossible bliss makes me feel disorientated
Conscious thought ends
Reality has stopped.
It is safe to be, safe to be,
Safe to be me below the waves.

Jason Aris

INSANE IN THEIR CAGES

Look at me,
take in my every twitch and quiver
watch me intently,
You'll see I'm stricken with psychosis
Absorb my madness
suck hard sweet child my sadness . . .

See how I rock,
machine like, laborious in motion
I'm a natural now,
For I'm nothing but your tired exhibition
My common sunrise
the legacy of yesterday's gawping faces . . .

I'm tired now,
my lethargy, the disdainful product of
being your curio,
Each day hangs like a sullen portrait
My mind a gallery
once exotica, turned dust covered freedom . . .

I see through Iron,
your wonderment, outshines your face
and my cold hysteria,
I . . . am less impressed at seeing you
Your presence bares
the jangling keys, for my faithful gaolers . . .

John C Kearney

LIBRAN

Leaves crackle as eager feet draw
the hooded figure deep into the heart
of the wood.
Barely containing his excitement
he envelopes his identity,
purges his inhibition,
pulls open the 'Barber' overcoat,
throws back the hood
and laughs

like a child on Christmas morning.
Arms wide, he greets the emerging branches
of each tree
as they shower their tender jewels
upon his avid, rejoicing form -
while grateful gaze ingests flight
of sycamore seeds, plunging 'conkers'
and fir cones which . . .
just drop.

Self-consciously he embraces
wonder - so imaginatively
called a tree -
pulling quickly, sheepishly away
at the sound of a distant whistle;
conscientious scan detects
no observers to judge him 'bonkers' -
just drunk with glee,
that's me!

Phoenix Martin

UNSOUND IN MIND

It starts as a whisper, that can hardly be heard.
Then it gets bugging, first second then third.
They are tiny squeaks, voices trapped in my head.
But when I awaken, these voices I dread.
Longing, waiting, pulsing, nagging, dying to be set free.
Why won't they let go? Will they just not let me be?
These voices rattle on, into deep long conversation.
They drip off my brain like acid condensation.
The voices tell me, to do things that I shouldn't.
Screaming, shouting, ranting, raving, want things I normally wouldn't
Sponge is my head, they seep through my brain.
Then cloud into one, like sludge down a drain.
They offer you help, to be put in a home
But I need more space, because I'm not alone.
They call you wild, like a cat you can't *tame*
But I'm not called me, I'm now called *insane* . . .

Georgette Hipwell

STOP, LOOK AND LISTEN

Time to Stop, Look around.
See the beauty of the world.

The blue of the sky,
White cotton wool clouds,
Sun! Moon! And stars so high.

The trees and flowers
Fields of green and gold,
Hills and valleys below,
Cattle and sheep grazing.

Listen - to the song of the birds.
The gaggle of the geese and buzz of the bees,
The ripple of the stream,
The whispering of the trees.

Church bells ring,
A baby's cry and laughter
As children play.
Oh! It's good to be alive, and
Take time to Listen
To God's words of love and peace.
Time to reflect and realise.
To appreciate the wonderful world
God has made for you and me, *but!*

This has been spoilt by *man*
Man has put noise and pollution on this world
From cars, trains, buses, motor-cycles,
Aeroplanes that roar in the sky.
Rockets, bombs and guns, man created these,
I prefer God's world for you and me,
Just *Stop, Look and Listen!*

Gladys Davenport

DEAD TREE AT SNIPE POINT

discarded by nature
pushed and pounded
by the violence of the sea
and abandoned high on the beach
this tree
carved by the elements
and bleached by the sun
provides a place of rest
a grandstand seat
from which to watch
the power of creation

a strong wind
pounds the waves
against the shattered
limestone edge
as dark rain clouds
hurry from the mainland
throwing hard pellets of rain
at my back

it's cold

and only the hardiest of birds
fly over the brooding sea
in search of food
while in this small haven
i sit and play
a low whistle tune
to re-unite
the living and the dead
and purge
my own ailing soul.

Keith Duke

THE BUILDING SITE (DEATH OF ADELPHI)

There used to be a building here
standing proud and ugly,
defiant to the passing sky.
Thousands waited for the call
within its velvet flocked walls,
that would make them rich.
There used to be a building here
where blue rinsed women
in floral print dresses
came to escape their
lives daily stresses
hoping for the big one on the card.
There used to be a building here
where people met and married, died
and lived, loved, laughed and cried.
Snapshots of clichéd humanity,
on Thursday nights and
twice weekly matinee.
There used to be a building here
but now it's only rubble
and due to be replaced in award winning style.
But something in glass and steel,
though architecturally aesthetic
won't have the same feel.
There will be another building here
but it will not be the same.
The poetry will have gone
and the people passing
will not have noticed.

Julian Bingham

WINTER SCENE

Winter trees black filigree
'Gainst blue and golden sky,
The grey of night advancing
As time goes scudding by.

Clouds show the pink of evening
As a white half moon appears,
Such lovely sights defying
The pain of passing years.

How many times have I seen such things,
How many hope to see,
Before time's advancing winter
Shall make an end of me.

L Beardsley

A GOLDEN MEMORY

You made your way through
striped umbrellas, where people
lay like starfish on the sand.
You came so close, beside me.
Your eyes were too familiar,
a startling shade of blue.

You spoke in a soft whisper
in foreign words that
I couldn't understand.
For a moment your eyes held mine,
and your fingers gently
touched my hand.

Maybe you were flirting with
me, feeling it was safe.
Then I saw the gold
cradled in your hand.
It was my Mother's ring
I'd lost in the sand.

My heart leaped,
I wanted you to stay.
But you turned and walked
to the edge of the sand
and looked out across
the bay.

In that moment, the whole beach
was bathed in a golden glare and
the sea, a sparkling plate of silver.
But then you were gone
and the brightness faded
with the last rays of the sun.

Anne Palmer

FOR THE LOVE OF A PRINCESS

What a shock the planet bore when the headlines hit the news
Everyone being blamed for her death, everyone airing their views
The nation mourned as never before
Bringing flowers and candles and tributes galore
They donated their money and gave of their time
Listened to broadcasts when the hour chimed
If tears were water there would never be drought
Oh what sadness her death's brought about
Dear Diana, The Princess of Wales
Every girl's Princess of fairy tales
Her popularity astounding beyond belief
They came by the thousand and many did grieve
From all walks of life the Mums and the Dads
The old and the young both lasses and lads
She was one in a million with a heart of gold
Though she's gone from this earth she will never grow old
A shining example to all whom she touched
The physical approach she loved it so much
William and Harry her devoted sons
Were raised very wisely I'm sure
Diana's influence in all that they do.
Will no doubt be honest and pure
Now that her funeral is over
And the coffin has been lain to rest
We shall always remember her fondly
She was 'Simply the Best'.

Valerie Morgan

SAY IT WITH FLOWERS

A bunch of flowers can say so much
When sent to someone with whom we've lost touch.
A vase of tulips can brighten our day
When placed in the church as we kneel and pray.
A posy of freesias can make someone glad
When she thinks of the garden she's never had.
A gift of flowers to someone who's ill
Will cheer them up more than any pill,
And a single red rose when lights are dim
Says more than a million words from him.
When you want to say, 'Sorry, I just didn't think.'
Then give her some flowers, and say with a wink
I hope you'll forgive me and make amends,
Let's kiss and make up and still be friends.
There's nothing as nice as a bride's bouquet
The finishing touch on her happiest day.
When troubles crop up and you're feeling forlorn
Just think of the rose and not of the thorn.
We take flowers to loved ones no longer here
And as we arrange them, perhaps shed a tear.
When words won't come, and you've pondered for hours
What nicer way than to say it with flowers.

Patricia A Cartwright

LOVE'S LIGHT

Dawn brings soft light that peeps thro' curtained night,
Soon, slanting beams beckon to waking earth,
Shadows vanish in explosions of light;
Sun's rise symbolises a new day's rebirth.
The light of my life, is love's steady flame;
In ever-widening circles stealing
In facets of awareness since you came.
Light is like truth, its brightness revealing.
If love dies, and sorrow smothers desire,
Myriads of stars will in heavens fade,
If a spark remains to kindle a fire
All is not lost; love's light will pervade.
I joyfully, and, with contented sighs
Will see my love reflected in your eyes.

Janet Newstead

DEATH

Death is but a breath away -
Suddenly it took a loved one today.
It came like a bolt out of the blue -
Accepting it is hard to do.
Shocked and stunned, I have grieved and cried,
I feel so numb, I ache inside.
Why? is the question that springs to mind,
There is no answer that I can find.
But, God in his wisdom has taken his hand
To guide him to the promised land.

Muriel E Read

SOLITUDE

Murky shadows on the wall,
My spirits rise, and then they fall.
Are you here, or far away?
Where did you go today?

Am I lost? Now I don't know.
Why love, did you have to go?
You're not here, to take my hand.
Why, oh, why, don't I understand?

At dawn there is another day.
Though you are a million miles away.
I am alone in my sorrow.
Just can't wait, until tomorrow.

Can I have my life again?
Did we do it all in vain?
Will you listen, to my plea
To take your chance, again with me?

Murky shadows on the wall.
My spirits rise, and then they fall.
Are you here or far away?
Where did you go today?

Sylvia Clark

I'M OPEN

You hold the door for me, why? Am I your girl? Your princess?
                                        Your forever?
Before I met you I only ever experienced desire . . .
Now I feel this sweet ache, which tingles my inner.
I want to explode - go wild - scream finally . . .
            I love you
I try restrain myself, consume my feelings and detach my every
                                        emotion. I cannot -
I just ache more, yearn more and love more.
I'm falling . . .
And scared . . .
Will you catch me?
My key I hid so well for so long
You found it
And used it
I'm open . . .
Am I your girl? Your princess? Your forever?
I close my eyes and enter my secret garden, only to find you
                there, waiting, holding my keys, forbidden no more.
Exception begins to play her violin melody, singing . . .
'He's yours and your his the only way to win is to open up completely.'

Marsha-Lee Barnes

EXPATRIATE BLUES

Sing, my love,
Of parted sorrow,
Counted weeks,
Slow tomorrow;
Phoned, feigned
Tranquillity.

Cry, my purse,
In growing thickness
Money shouts
Future frailties,
Pauperised
Timidity.

False, my smile
Aching lonesome
Eighty days
Without home-come
Financial need,
Exigency.

Weep, my heart,
Sundered, glooming,
Votive years
Slowly looming
Sterile end,
Solitary.

Andrew Wareham

TINCTURE

It is quiet in here.
It is as though the air hangs breathless, on the point of expectation.
I whisper and hear no echo of the hush and hiss of my voice.
Softly, softly,
Do not disturb this barren peace.
Do not halt this hibernation.

Morning is coming again. It serves to cauterise the room.
I must leave the room.
Crucified at the window; instil my whole body with light.
No, no, do not crumple,
Maintain the pose.
Give me the energy, it is needed.

Distract me now that the darkness is gone,
Lead me astray,
Alter my perception, stop me thinking.
Useless, useless. You just stare blankly,
Staying sufficiently to bisect hope
Then gone before time.

It is quiet again;
Mausoleum-like and I am tightly curled.
Faded; there is no remnant or calling card.
Hush, hush,
The breathing disturbs me,
And I am left waiting, waiting.

Danny Lewis

RAINDROPS

A raindrop falls a clear blue
From the open sky into a scented room.

A scenic sun bellows rays of light
Nightmare that fades, from the night.

Tranquillity evolves my passionate soul
With the dice of life, the winning roll.

A raindrop falls to a river deep
Strength that grows, from morning, until I sleep.

A craving of lustfulness lays awake
My arms caress, your body I take.

Arouse my mind and stimulate my heart
Enlighten my aura, to be seen from afar.

Your fruits of love delight with pleasure
You are my soul, my love, my treasure.

Our bodies entangled as the moonlight shines
A dream that rages into the night.

A raindrop reflection gleams from the eye
A twinkling star beams bright in the sky

Lips that kiss so sweet, so pure
I have the addiction, you are the cure.

Lightning that strikes, explosion of thunder
My light, my raindrops, my eighth wonder.

Paul Axtell

MAN BREAD HORSE

Saturday revenant
Mr Law/the bread man/one arm and wicker
Basket/shafts of odour/the horse-bit

Levels of light
History cut now and then/the grave-capped
Heliograph of here and no

Husk to the front and mind back
(Spatter thro' windows an inner slide
....the blur then)

Impregnation
Of syllable silence, meaning
Spectres and true myth

The last Georgian infancy;
Sunk in a town's heart. The play of life,
Ourselves as morning parts.

Hugh Allott

OUT OF REACH

Rustling leaves and bending branches
Giving way to passing breezes,
In momentary glances
Then so still it almost freezes.

Sunlight dappled gently
So quiet in its intrusion,
On the place I sit intently
In peaceful exclusion.

Wilderness surrounds me
But I fear nothing from this place,
Nature in its entirety
So warm in its embrace.

The river bends the rushes
They give to its persuasion,
It pulls and it pushes
With its rippling invasion.

This will remain an untouched place
As nature has intended,
As long as from the human race
It will be well defended.

J Howson

SONG FOR BOBBY

Out of the blue
  come whispers and arrows;
dust falls through blue light.
The livid sound of days cracks open:
one after another falling
  from the frame.
A film plays background
to your hours
and from the night
  dreams pass into day.

P Gwilliam

SEASHORE

Wave-dappled sand, smoothly inviting
Small naked footprints etched in your breast
Circling seabirds in pairs are alighting
On cliff face, and rock, to establish a nest
Driftwood, and seaweed, washed up by the high tide
Tossed to and fro on your way to the shore
Loud plaintive call as a solitary gull cries
Turning its smooth wings seaward once more.

Turbulent ocean, your sea horses leaping
Curly white manes plunging forward in line
Eager and lively, their ranks ever keeping
Washing the shore with their salt-laden brine.
Tossing and turning, swirling together
Sometimes quite docile, others so wild
Frothy white sea horses which no hand can tether
Break into foam at the foot of a child.

Irene Hustwait

PEACE

The perfume from the meadow and the trees
Comes wafting to me on the gentle breeze
The humming insects suckling on honeyed flowers
Invade my ears and fill my lonely hours
The silvered leaves upon the full-grown birch
Caress my eyes; and in the distant church
The bells ring out, inviting all to pray
And give a humble thank you for this day.
The winding lane with hedgerows on each side
Abundant with all little things that hide
Beneath their leaves, a hollow at their root
A tiny mouse inside a cast-off boot
I watch the rabbits as they skip and play
Also the rippling river on its way
A grassy cushion soft beneath my feet
Under a shady tree where lovers meet
I see it now, and stare with different eyes
From those once dimmed with sadness of goodbyes
For now at last you're home with me to stay
And peace is now forever more, we pray.

Helen M Hyatt

THE OLD PATCHWORK QUILT

It is waiting to be mended, to be given a new life,
That patchwork quilt that Mum made as a young and thrifty wife.
When first she started courting she decided she would try
To make a bedspread for her bottom drawer, by and by.

She didn't need to go and buy the patchwork squares those days,
Her mother fashioned clothes for all the family, she says,
Mum simply begged some offcuts from pyjamas, shirt and dress,
Then snipped around to make them join each other - more or less!

She didn't cut them all to size - there was no great design,
But all was new and all came free and all looked very fine,
And best of all, each piece reminded Mum of someone dear,
What memories that quilt would stir through many a happy year!

She was away in service and had one day off each week,
A twelve-mile cycle ride back home, but always she would seek
To find the time that day to add a little loving touch
To that fascinating bedspread which still we love so much.

Over the years the patchwork grew, the happy couple wed,
They furnished well their little home and soon upon the bed
Was laid that splendid cover, sewn with love in every stitch,
They couldn't buy a better one - even if they'd been rich!

It is waiting to be mended, to be renewed once more:
It looks quite well considering this year it's sixty four.
No question of its being pensioned off at sixty five,
I'll patch, enjoy and cherish it as long as I'm alive!

Margaret Sanders

JUST LIKE GRANDMA

Grandma, I don't want to go to bed
Can I stay a while, with you instead
I promise I won't wake the boys
I will play quietly with my toys.

So Sara and I played for a while
I must admit she made me smile
When she climbed up on my knee
She reminded me how I used to be.

I was Grandma's special girl too
There were things she'd let me do
Together we had lots of fun
I think like her I have become.

Read me a story Sara said
Before I could she was asleep instead
My, she's heavy now she's four
Thank goodness Grandad's coming through the door.

Now dear Sara's tucked safely in bed
Many the thoughts that are in my head
I'm sure a good Grandma Sara will make
If after me dear Sara will take.

R Lee

THE LAST PARISH
(For Marion and Kevin)

On this sun-dappled seascape
       Let your observation dwell
Upon Great Blasket riding
       Proud upon a ruffled swell,
While pinnacles of Tearacht
       Thrusting from the ocean floor,
Rear jagged opposition
       To the broad Atlantic's maw.

Yet do not idly welcome
       What your eyes now feast upon,
These isles appear idyllic
       But the islanders have gone.
A humble folk were starved out
       By the elements they fought
To wrest a meagre living
       That was often dearly bought.

Those times are past forever
       And I think it's for the best,
Their panoramic photos
       Leave a part of me depressed.
Each face, carved with endurance,
       Gazes, weather-worn, but set
Upon a lost horizon,
       And the Blaskets are there yet.

Jim Finch

BALLET DREAMS

My inner thoughts I will betray
I dream to play lead in the corps de ballet
Oh how I wish to prance and dance
And throw myself about like a lance
To wear tight hose
That would my manliness disclose
And well contoured underneath
I would wear a codpiece MX at least
For young ladies to delight
And young men to observe nature's slight
On stage to ballerinas I will haste
On tiptoe but well-paced
And I would throw around
Young girls by the kilo and pound
Into the air then I would leap
Flutter as a bird and land in a heap.
But your fears I will allay
For my wishes will as dreams stay
But if ever I should be reincarnated
My dreams would be as afore stated.

Brian Norman

LABOUR OF LOVE

'The garden's a mess, it needs a man's hand'
My other half said 'Go till the land.'
Reluctant but resigned to the garage I wander
A jumbled mess, too much to ponder,
Spade and fork, rake and push mower,
Not very smart but it's still a goer.

That's sorted the kit it looks nice and tidy,
But look at the garden, it'll take till next Friday
Mow the lawn and trim all the hedges,
Hoe down the rows, but mind the veggies,
The moss on the lawn, I must use the rake,
That looks somewhat better but my back does ache.

The flowers look great, red, yellow and blue,
Rainbow colours, yes of every hue,
Apples and pears all manner of fruit,
Peas and beans, carrots, even beetroot,
All growing together in my little plot.
I like it, I like it, I like it a lot.

Ah, here comes the wife, she'll show her delight,
She will be impressed at the nice tidy sight,
'Well, not bad, but the lawn needs a roll'
I sense a sneeze getting out of control
Some small insect or pollen from a rose?
No! Just my dearly-beloved, got right up my nose.

A Walker

A World Of My Own . . .

I wish I could live on a great big star
that twinkled in the sky
where the Garden of Eden was more than a dream
where the angels really fly

I wish I could live on a great big star
that sailed through the heavens so blue
where peace would reign for evermore
our troubles be but few

I wish I could live on a great big star
that had never heard of war
where there were no lies no ugly thoughts
each heart an open door

I wish I could live on a great big star
where my wishes would all come true
for only then on a world of my own
will it be as I want it to.

John E Barnard

IF I COME BACK!

I'd like to come back as an eagle,
if somehow, I were given the choice.
Or, a lion in the African jungle,
with a bellowing roar, for a voice.

As an eagle, I'd soar to the heavens,
reaching inaccessible heights.
Held in the air by elegant wings,
enjoying my solitary flights.

With hardly a foe trying to hurt me,
and a mate that is mine, throughout life.
Just imagine the feeling it must be,
to be flying there, free, without strife!

Or, if I came back as a lion,
my feet would be firm on the ground.
I'd be known as the King of the Jungle,
and would keep all my 'pride', safe and sound.

But, supposing my thoughts of returning,
do not go quite according to plan!
Say I'm sent back as something real tasty,
to be hunted, then eaten, by man!

Pauline Jones

HOPE

It soon died.
   Long ago I believed
I'd meet her again.
   In a busy street,
On the London tube,
   Or, perhaps, spot
Her likeness in a
   Newspaper picture -
Hopefully still single.

It soon died.
   This thing called Hope.

But in dreams
   A piece of string,
If that be Hope,
   Might be long enough
To reach the stars . . .

Simon Morton

CONCERN

Bugs and butterflies
Worms and moths
That as children we stepped upon
As we were running fast across the park
Down to the river
To feed the ducks.

In those our early years
We noticed not our accidental wrath
Nor the creatures' sad predicaments.

We were too busy
Smiling into the sunshine
Running to the squash and sandwiches.

It's only when
We come a cropper

That we notice
The poor grasshopper.

And closely consider
The little things
Even those that bite
And sting.

Meg Gunner

A NEW LINK

Grandma (that's me) - a name that's new,
Though heard in dreams a thousand times.
Warm mini-fingers round my thumb
And common phrases dance in rhymes!

I walk beside the windowpane,
My grin reflected all the way.
Those cancers didn't stand a chance
- I *had* to live to see today!

Cell upon cell, unseen by eye,
Life's blueprint once again obeyed -
A perfect link to join Life's chain,
Stretched whole from Eve to Lois Jade.

My genes are yours to guard, my love,
Long past the day when we must part,
For I will live while you still breathe.
My daughter's daughter holds my heart.

Oh, may you know this joy, my dear,
When years have flown and you are old.
In tiny eyes that look like yours
You'll understand the tales I've told.

Let life be full and hearts be true
And love will make the chain stay whole.
Then, in the evening mists, you'll feel
Your children's children thrill your soul.

Jenny Whiteside

FAREWELL TO A FRIEND

It was a '39 Austin - FKH 107,
It had been up to Glasgow and down to Devon,
Yes - it was mine, my very first car,
I was really quite proud of my old 'jam jar'.
Good old banger!

It used to stand there, battered and worn,
Looking rather bedraggled and rather forlorn,
It had seen some good service and gone round the clock,
But now struggled hard to get round the block,
Did my banger!

The wings were bent, the exhaust very rusty,
And inside it was just a little bit musty,
The steering pulled left, and then right to one side,
And the brakes didn't stop very well when applied,
On my banger!

However the engine had a heart of gold,
Chugged merrily along, although it was old,
And motoring went by without a hitch,
Until one day I skidded into a ditch,
Poor old banger!

It was badly bruised when they pulled it clear,
Somewhat more buckled and bent at the rear,
Then we limped sadly off and back to the garage,
To learn the worst about the damage,
To my banger!

My faithful transport had run its last mile,
And now it was just a name on a file.
Down at the yard - as they winched it up high,
Did I hear a wistful parting sigh
From my banger!

Brian Fisher

ACCIDENT

Storm, clattering thunder, dazzling flame sword
The weather brought weak trees down
Rasping, exposed arms swayed as if possessed.

Screeching car, loud crackling branch
A victim, haunted with these sounds in sleep
The white chalk marks in the road
Soon disappeared with traffic and rainfall.

His thirst for life is fading
On wind's dead leaves pirouetted then disappeared.
His dad collected the branch
Chopped, tied into neat bundles for firewood.
No one mentions the storm now.

The son sits warming himself
Daydreams he's at a limb-loss funeral
His void so dark and inward
Pretends ash from his dead limb is close by.

Stares into the red-hot flame,
His lost limb the awkward amputation
The dreams and hopes he strived for.

Marisha Rose

THE CHRISTMAS WE DON'T DREAM OF

Somewhere out there,
In the cold night air,
Lies a country at war,
Needing peace much more
At Christmas time.

They flee and die,
Side by side.
No presents at all,
No tree, so tall,
At Christmas time.

Families are split apart,
Which breaks their hearts.
They are hungry and cold.
They won't live to be very old
At Christmas time.

We're joyful and glad,
They're lonely and sad.
Can't we stop this hatred,
Surely life's too sacred,
At Christmas time.

Chloé Sharrocks (12)

GIRL

The Human Sacrifice skips sweetly forward,
Dancing the path of naiveté, holding her lover's hand.
Reputation is the first to go.
She must become known as *His*,
She must let her identity grow and attach
Itself to him.

The words of the Human Sacrifice are heavy
With herself. Bit by bit he absorbs her.
She tells him of her thoughts and feelings.
She tells him that she loves him,

And he echoes, she sees a reflection of her
Love in his eyes, and sighs with joy.
For indeed; he does love the gap she fills.

Eventually he has taken her, soul, heart and body,
(Although he leaves her a little indigestible mind)
And he is full.

So there is nothing more, and
The Human Sacrifice must leave the table.

Whilst the dish she was served up on was sparkling bright,
She remains dirty to the core, dying, dying.

The sorry sight of the Human Sacrifice
Hides behind her fingers,
And watches the next course.

As he devours another identity, a new offering
From the school of innocents,
She cracks.

All that is left is a blinking eye
That watches her replacement and
Bathes relentlessly in its last offerings.

When he has spat out the mouldy dust of her memory,
She picks it up from the floor,
And tries to pull herself together.

Christy Wyatt

NATURE'S CATHEDRAL

While taking a walk in the country
One fine Sunday morning
I heard the church bells pealing
Calling the faithful to worship
A sense of guilt overcame me
Should I not be joining them?
I then realised, I was more fortunate
For I was in nature's Cathedral.
The green lush grass of the forest paths
Was more soft than any carpeted aisle
The sturdy oaks became the pillars
The rocks, the pulpit and the altar.
Pretty flowers of many a hue
Compared equally to any stained-glass window.
The birds' song as sweet as any choir's offering.
The rockpool, a font became.
When I raised my eyes
The sun and the clouds in the blue sky
Formed a glorious ceiling
Surpassing any Michaelangelo painting.
My guilt vanished
For I felt nearer to God in these surroundings
Than I would sitting in any church
Built by man alone.

Jacqueline Taylor

THE SEA

My silhouette became an explorer,
Surrounded by nature's night light.
One's thoughts were oblivious,
To any other sight.

I began to breath in deeply,
As the air felt filtered fresh.
The swoop of angels' kisses,
Blew through my dress.

Freshly picked seaweed became captured,
Between my toes.
Sounds of quailing dolphins,
Faintly echoed.

Gushes of great waves,
Splashed between my legs,
Awaiting for pollution,
To raise its ugly head.

Relaxed by the melting moon,
Exhilarated by the ocean's smell.
A taste for the seafront,
Is something for what I dwell.

Hayley Edwards

Untitled

I shall love you forever
No matter where
No matter when

I shall hold you
In my heart
And hope we meet again.

Some feelings never die
Although they may not shine
They remain in the shadow
The place where you are mine.

Jeanne Barczewska

THE NEW DAWN

As humanity flicks over the page,
Opens the door at the dawn of an age,
Will it bring peace and goodwill to men,
Or more the same, again and again?

Will we heed the warning,
Put an end to global warming,
Save the forests and the seas,
Or pollute however we please?

What about the panda, the tiger, the whale
Don't say we're going to fail,
To save proud creatures from extinction,
Won't we have achieved great distinction?

Is it all about an aluminium dome,
Which will become the ephemeral home,
To our materialistic treasure,
And our passing pleasure?

Will we hold each other hand in hand,
Bring peace to Ireland, the Holy Land,
Or will we shoot, bomb and blast,
As it's ever been through our past?

As humanity sees that new dawn,
Is the hope too forlorn,
That two thousand years from Jesus' birth,
There'll be lasting peace throughout the earth?

Alan Flockton

MILLENNIUM MAN

Young and goofy School's a drag,
Bunking off to have a fag.
Fashion passion, dress the part.
Blow the mind and fire the heart.
Smoking, Poking, 'Play the field'.
Assertive. Argue. Never yield
Some would claim a purpose here,
That's quite apart from fags and beer.
As in all logic, there's a hitch
They're either very young or rich.
Belt and waistband getting bigger,
Have a pint and *sod* the figure!
Youthless, Toothless, Life is flat.
You live, you die, and that is that!

Anthony D Parker

HOW DO I LOVE YOU?

I love you as much
as a lawyer loves fees
and I think of you as often
as a mouse thinks of cheese

You make my heart light
like a leaf on a breeze
and to my thoughts and emotions
you hold all the keys

Your warmth could demolish
a midwinter freeze
and when I think of your kiss
I go weak at the knees

You give me more buzz
than a hive full of bees
and if you went I would miss you
as much as birds would miss trees

Knowing you love me
puts my senses at ease
Please love me forever
please darling please
For I'll always love you
in ways such as these.

Stan Jenkins

ARACHNOPHOBIA

A spider on my ceiling,
Another on my wall,
I'm feeling spider-phobic,
But why? They are *so* small!

They'll crawl into my bed, through my ears, into my head.
They'll bite me, lay their eggs, a million spiders in my legs.
And so, to end my strife I fear I'll have to take a life - or two!

No spiders on my ceiling,
No spiders on my wall,
I am completely spiderless,
'Goodnight' - after all!

Lisa Sones

LAST FAG AT RANGOON

Liberated,
Homeward bound,
On a stretcher,
In the shade of a Dakota's wing.
Half a Woodbine,
Clenched between broken teeth
And ulcerated lips.
Yellowed fingers
Of a skeletal hand,
Blistered, trembling,
Too weak to remove it.
A sigh of weariness,
Then the faint, rattling gasp
Of one last intake of breath
To fuel the glowing cigarette tip
Into a rosy setting sun
On his youthful life.
The ash grows longer,
A smoky wraith
Helter-skelters silently
To a cobalt sky,
A tenuous Indian rope
For his freed soul
To climb up to
The gilded wrought iron
Of the Pearly Gates,
Through which it gently swirls
Into a soldier's heaven.

John Martin

ZOE

Sunrise, sunset, I dream of you
An Enchantress of
endless loveliness.

Dazzling your smile, a breathtaking
gift you bestow to me.

How enchanting your sapphire eyes
of sparkling splendour.

Your ruby hair of flowing silk,
An elegant touch to your
prettiness.

Softness is your face, akin petals
of a thousand roses.

Softly, sweet your enchanting
voice, a melody of poetry.

An everlasting wish
you are to Me.

Sho S C Tang

THE IRIS

In the long tall grass,
a splash of colour shows through,
catching our eye as we pass
is the Iris with its rich shades of blue.

It grows by a river or a stream,
somewhere not to spoil,
a place to sit and dream,
or admire its indigo and royal.

Like a beautiful ball gown,
so proud and elegant,
a sapphire in nature's crown,
the Iris so resplendent.

Heather Pfander

UNTITLED

I glance down . . . there it is
Just tossed on the floor
He thinks it will stop
The tears waiting to pour

Such a beautiful sight
My heart starts to melt
Forgetting the pain
And the anger I've felt

A scent so divine
Its aroma cries out
To the love in my heart
Casting out all the doubt

I look in his eyes
Is that honesty there?
Or a well hidden lie
To make sure I still care?

I smile and we kiss
My love steadily flows
Forgiven . . . forgotten . . .
All it took was a rose.

Karen Horne

THE TOWER

In the darkness,
I lay on this bed I've made,
Trying to believe, that one day
things might change.

Yes, I'm lonely inside,
Behind these walls I've made,
I built them brick by brick,
until I was enslaved.

This silence is my prison,
These chains are my own tears,
I feel the pain for a reason,
that's been killing me for years.

I look out of my tower,
I see the princes riding by,
I just sit alone for hours,
just asking myself why.

I used to have some colours,
Of blue and red and gold,
But now they are all worthless,
tattered, faded and old.

I know that one day I shall
Slowly climb down from here,
Shouting that I'm not afraid
and wiping away the tears.

In the darkness,
I see my clock, the hours are long,
I'm still here wondering,
where the hell I went wrong!

Marie Souza

WINTER MOON

Moonlight spills on tree and hollow
Owl sits dark against the sky
Silent mist steals across the meadow
Soft purring wings, small animal cry.

Cobwebs kissed with crystal tears
Hang like garlands from each tree
Reflections in the ice-bright water,
Catch moon's face as she rides free.

J Branney

TRAVELLING COMPANIONS

Silently travelling - nothing to say
As we speed along the motorway
Quietly sitting side by side
Through miles and miles of countryside.

No need for words - I know him so well
His every thought and mood I can tell.
Two souls in quiet communion
A contented, peaceful union.

In much the same way we travel through life
Side by side as man and wife
Carefully planning the route we take
Unaware of the changes the Lord will make.

Iris White

THE EMPTY HOUSE

Come see my empty house!
It has no love or beat therein.
For all its gaiety and sin,
Without me now to grumble and grouse.

The windows stare like empty eyes,
But look at you, so deep within
And see your sorrow, unrequited now.
Tell me, what's in your heart?
No more fear, no more lies!

The door never now beckons,
It doesn't hold the promise to you
Of happier days when you were young.
Tho' life's troubles were not few.

Now is the chain that binds us, unbroken,
Love given to me is just a token,
On memories fading we have to dwell,
For forgiveness, our souls we'll sell.

Be not afraid, ere love will find
A way to hold all dreams and bind.
Was I in love, all those years ago?
Did I argue sometimes, with 'so and so'?

Did I hurt you at some early time?
For this I beg you, forgive me,
As I forgive the ones, who to me
Were not so fine!

All love transcends the hurts,
But not in this old house!
Where love and faith now deserts
Where now is missed
The other spouse!

Sans breath! Sans love! Sans family!

Ray Gordon-Tilley

ODE TO OUR DOCTORS AND NURSES

The sleep of the night is now shattered
That's the sound of the ambulance bell,
The doctors and nurses are rushing
To What - they just cannot tell

It could be a multi-car pile-up
With nine or ten people involved
Each needing experienced attention
Before their problems are solved

It could be an elderly person
To whom the last call has just come
In the low early hours of the morning
Saying life's journey on earth is now done

It could be a wife who's expecting
The joy of a child to bring forth
A long-awaited desire;
So completing her marriage troth

It could be a besotted drug addict
Deranged and out of his mind
Fighting and screaming his hatred
Of them and all of mankind

But whatever they find in 'Admittance'
Our medical teams work on -
In the early hours of the morning
Till their mercy work is all done

May God bless our doctors and nurses
Self-giving in all that they do;
Relieving much pain and suffering
Their caring and love shining through.

Enid Holmes

A LETTER POEM FOR YOU

I'm sending you a letter,
written in the language of my smiles.
I attach
the fingerprints of my happiness,
the throbbing of my heart,
and a sample of my love.
Please, test it thoroughly
under the microscope of your soul.

Gregory Baczewski

REMINDING ME

Peeping from underneath a cloud
The sun shouts out aloud
Summer skies, so very blue
Reminding me once more of you.
Your eyes, how you looked, and
Moved with grace.
The sunshine on your beautiful face
And hair that shone like glistening dew.

J J Collins

TREE FREE

Yellow beasts of mass destruction
fulfil the planners' needs,
another scheme designed to free
the traffic from our city streets.

Yellow beasts of mass destruction
fulfil the planners' dreams
another road designed to free
our countryside of fields and trees.

S R Vincent

EMPTY ECHOES

If only I could light a flame,
For people out there who have a name,
My warning words fly on the winds,
To be caught, only, by ears as fins.

Doubtless, most would shut them out,
Here, the wise, would have to shout,
In the shouting echoes call,
Onto deaf ears, words would fall.

As all echoes, long and loud,
Miss the target, miss the crowd,
What's the purpose? What's the use?
That! You'll find is the mind's excuse.

They do not heed, the mind, I feed,
I slow, as drought waters flow,
Pity the many who do not see,
So, my words, bounce back to me.

E B Whitmore

THE VISIT

The driveway is winding and wooded each side,
a clearing appears there are lawns far and wide.
Borders of flowers all tended with care,
the like of which would be hard to compare.
There stands the house so stately and proud,
it opens its doors to the chattering crowd.
Voices are hushed as we pass on inside,
like sheep with their shepherd we stay close to our guide.
Pictures and portraits gaze down from the walls,
magnificent tapestries line the great halls.
The ballroom so splendid brings gasps of delight,
all golden and white lit by candles at night.
When the flames are extinguished so the story is told,
a ghost may be seen arms outstretched to enfold.
She searches in vain for the love that's no more,
it's said that he never returned home from war.

We have stepped back in time as we listen in awe,
of treachery and murder and more country lore.
Moving onto the bedrooms where four poster beds,
stand swathed in fine drapes, lace pillows at their heads.
These walls have been privy to romance and intrigue,
they hold on to secrets never to concede.
A look below stairs soon dispels all the magic,
hard working servants their lives dull and tragic.
Serving their masters knowing their place,
then leaving this earth soon are lost without trace.
The visit was over and questions were asked,
we compared modern lifestyle with that of the past.
Then we left the old house with its legend and treasure,
holding on to the memory of a day filled with pleasure.

Margaret Wilson

TIME MOVES ON

The dinosaurs used to roam these lands,
Millions of years ago,
They dwindled away one by one,
But still time moved on.

Mammals have survived so far,
for how long one does not know,
If you take a look around you,
you might wonder how.
For every resource this world has,
is disappearing one by one,
But still time moves on.

Most of our wildlife is becoming extinct,
Forests are being cut down,
We are polluting the land, sea and air.
But do we really care,
That every resource known to man is -
disappearing one by one?
No, because time still moves on.

Half of the world's people are starving,
because food supplies are so low,
Human greed has become too much,
And is now beginning to show,
But still time moves on.

We must start to save on resources,
Look after what we have,
This may well be our last chance,
We could end up like the dinosaurs,
And dwindle one by one,
But still time will move on,
Without us.

K Richardson

MY FRIENDS THEY TELL ME

My friends they tell me of their wives and how
They've aged; how time has robbed them of their looks
And grace that one-time to the marriage vow
Impelled. I listen to a catalogue of faults:
Of fattening waists and thickening arms and thighs
And all that stirred their youthful hearts to dance -
Now no more than a wistful dream that sighs
The loss of vanished slender-figured elegance.

And musing on this matrimonial woe
A youth-possessing image floods my mind -
Of her who never can be subject to
The cruelties of age, nor habit ever fade
That comely grace that once enraptured me -
Locked in the time-chest of my memory.

Philip Sanders

TEDDY
(For Lesley, then aged 7 years)

He's black and white
And I cuddle him tight
When underneath the blankets
I snuggle at night
He's getting old now
But I do love him so!
He's been to the seaside
And to the zoo
For wherever I go
Teddy goes too.
I tell him when I'm happy
And when I'm sad
Teddy's the best friend
That I've ever had.
I hope I don't lose him
For we never could part
If I lost teddy, it would break my heart
For then I'd have no one
To take to the park.
When I'm grown, I'll not let him go
Dear old teddy
I'll still love him so.
With his old battered face
He'll take pride of place
Along with the books
On top of my bookcase.

Irene G Corbett

LOVE'S NOT TIME'S FOOL!

As I have looked these forty years and more,
       I looked upon the face of my true love
And felt the blood course faster thro' my veins
       Just as it did when I first saw that face
Which changed my life so very long ago;
       I felt the years slip off my ageing back -
My aching limbs seemed not to burden me,
       I'm young again whene'er I look upon
That kindly face, as when my eyes first fell
       Upon that vision of delight, that dream
That's with me yet, and will be, all my life!
       Looking on that old familiar face
I notice not the wrinkles planted there
       By time's rough hand, but only see the girl
To whom I lost my heart. Yes, even should
       Our years advance to top the century
And we both wear old age's grotesque mask,
       And tho' we look like living skeletons,
Yet will I look, as I have looked before
       On that beloved face, and feel the blood
Course faster thro' my veins - just as of yore!
       Though haggard lines disfigure her good looks
And beauty's rose a wither'd flower be,
       I'll look upon her faded cheek, and see,
Not time's decay - but true love's immortality.

P A Robinson

THE FINAL STRAW

The final straw of bitterness
within their love - once sweetly blessed,
unfolded, hard with disbelief
when she announced she was to leave

because the loving tenderness
had grown throughout the years less.
She vowed that it was for the best . . .
As sadly, then, began to weave
The final straw.

She turned and asked him if he'd guessed
about her brief affair - and yes -
with tears, he said he'd too deceived,
but now her love was all he breathed.
And with a kiss, they laid to rest
The final straw.

Lynda Ann Green

THE LIGHT STEPS OUT

The night trembles before it wakes,
I move away from the place we built
before it's too late;
A shadow stirs, a light steps out
moves into the foreground
when no one else's about;
Your face, your ever-increasing needs,
warning shots are fired
that bring me to my knees;
The daylight breaks a heart
as the view pans out,
here is where you are
and the light steps out.

Le Fort

YIN AND YANG

My grandma . . . bless her cotton socks,
is ninety-six today,
and never fails to bend my ear,
so I just let her say,
'bout how the world's so violent,
drunken thugs upon the bus,
least nowadays we don't have 'itler . . .
dropping bombs on us!

Ah yes . . . here comes the one about
the bobby down the street,
with campaign ribbons on his chest,
and size twelve boots on feet,
went to fight the Krauts in France,
'cause Kitchener thought it right,
but he can't hear him crying, screaming,
each and every night.

Yup . . . life was far more pleasant then,
no AIDS, drugs, flying pickets,
just mass depression, Jarrow marchers,
TB and childhood rickets!
The gospel according to St Nan is . . .
'Britain lost the Great,
when Bevan opened up his trap,
and spoke of the welfare state'.

As you can tell, this argument,
could run for quite some time,
until hell hath frozen up . . . or
when the words don't rhyme!
Now as the curtain starts to fall,
I say to my gran'mother,
'What a world we all could build,
if we learn from each other.'

Pete Nash

THE VINTAGE YEARS

It is said that in old age
One matures like a good wine
But not until the bottle is uncorked
Can one say the taste is fine

Many a good vintage wine
If not kept in a good cellar
Can give the drinker a taste
Of something akin to vinegar

Wine comes in a variety of bottles
Of different colours and shapes
And sometimes there is a feeling
It is the product of sour grapes

When old age is compared to wine
The choice is from plonk to Kabinet
And the label on every bottle
Indicates the flavour and bouquet

If I must be compared to wine
I hope for a fine vineyard name
And I would like to retain the sparkle
Of a good year in champagne —

K W Benoy

MEN AT WORK

Industrial wounds in your green sides
Does the pain linger yet where they tore
At your secret and unseen places?
They have covered your scars
With monsters of greyness and grime
That huddle in ugliness,
And with remorseless fingers
Strangle the flowers that would
Cover your agonies,
Do they know they are death as they spread
A grey cloud over the skies
That worshipped your running waters?
And have they souls to feel
As they lie there with their creators
Sucking your shrivelled breasts?
Did they know they had souls
Before they opened their eyes
Onto the gritty darkness?
Or do they sometimes remember,
And moan in the twilight hours,
As inherited memory stirs
Your long forgotten voices?
Then the slug hand reaches and numbs them
And so they live without pain
Ever pushing them onward,
Living a life more dead than their death
When they lie in your soft and welcoming bosom
Oh, these are the saddest
The worst created things.

Barbara L Fisher

WINDOW

Through my window
Houses, all gleaming and new
A neighbourhood born
From a meadow that once grew

Harmless by day
Menacing by night
Voices come beaming
More threatening than bright

Through the window
Behind the nets
I sit and watch
What's passing next

Dog and a woman
Who's walking who?
Sniffing the floor
For what has passed through

Cars fly by on errands
On speed and on gas
People boxed in
By their own piece of glass

Children at play
Where's their watchful eye?
How long before they touch
The cars as they fly?

Girl and boy, holding hands
Through a summer haze
Oh, for the moment,
Remembering those days

Through my window what do I see?
I see my reflection staring back at me.

P Roche

JAMAICA

Cloudless, clear azure skies create a shimmering heat haze,
Underneath which the pure, light, yellow-brown beaches
Entice you to embrace this living Garden of Eden!
The island abounds with luscious rich forests thronged with tall
palm trees and iridescent greenery.
Clear, virgin rivers rush to the open sea over the rocks, pools and
beautiful beaches.
The aquamarine sea teems with multicoloured game fish, creating a
myriad rainbow.
Further inland, the fertile plains yield vast crops of banana, coconut
and sugar cane.
Peopled with vibrant, exciting, friendly locals with lilting voices.
Brown, black, pink with all shades of sepia thrown in,
The Jamaicans live in close, near-perfect racial harmony.
Warm tropical nights laced with ice-cold white rum let the
imagination run riot,
Bringing to the mind crystal clear images of buccaneers, Lords of
England, plantation revelry and the bewigged moustached Henry
Morgan
for which this vacation paradise is famed.
Well preserved, grand historic houses add to this imagery conjuring
up a sense of déjà vu.
Jamaica, like the Bacardi and Malibu adverts, lives up to its reputation.
As I board my plane, I think to myself when will I next feel your
warm, tender caress?

Robin Halder

SEARCHING FOR SOMETHING BETTER

Stuck in a seemingly endless rut,
A life more ordinary.
Every day is the same,
Nothing changes; it just kills me,
A slow lingering boring death.

A routine cemented in place,
Same work, same play.
Nothing interesting or exciting happens.
I feel I've seen it all before,
But back then it was better.

I feel like I'm the only one like this,
The others are happy in their lives,
In love with the familiar.
They don't see the shackles,
Or don't care about them.

I have to climb out of this rut,
Before I suffocate and die.
The mundane is bringing me down.
I need excitement and variation
To make me feel alive.

I need to cut the strings that tie me
So I can run from here,
And take a leap into the unknown,
Living for kicks, feeding my mind
Instead of choking in sameness.

Daniel Parton

DAD

Dad had the sparkle of life,
No trouble and strife,
For life is a four letter word
As far as I'm concerned.
Cruelly taken away
For he could no longer stay,
Mum kept him alive,
She loved him more and more to make him survive.
Love was the thing to keep them together
For they vowed forever and ever.
In sickness and in health
Through poverty and wealth
He left this world to ease his pain,
We knew it would never be the same.
Thankfully we have our mother,
Myself and my brother,
She gives everything she can
To replace the only man,
The man who made her laugh,
The man who made her cry,
She hoped that he would never, ever die.
They say that there is a reason,
I think it's all treason,
To leave the ones you love,
To float in the skies above,
Life must go on,
To prove that it is no con.
With love to a dad,
Who could never, ever be bad.

Paula Buck

THE AIR CHANGES

The air changes,
Grows heavy,

Seems to hang down in bunches,
Like grapes or wild cherries.

And the stone,
Each inward breath makes its own,

Wears down through time
The other's hardness.

Dominic Price

AUTUMN

How lovely are the colours
That greet me on this autumn morn
The trees stand so majestic
Bedecked in green and yellow and
Bronze and copper
This world to adorn

The sun glints through
A bluish haze
This sight it truly
Does me amaze
The hedgerows and cotoneaster are ablaze
With scarlet berries
To light up the land
Just another touch
Of the master's hand

The winds are getting sharper now
And leaves begin to
Rustle and fall and float and drift
from the bough

The pathways and the parklands everywhere
Are strewn with leaves
And thick carpets of leaves
Encircle the trees
A grey mantle now hangs over all
Will winter be here I
Wonder with tomorrow's dawn

Margaret A Stonier

NOVEMBER SUNDAY
(The walk to Highley)

Last train back to Kidderminster,
      the Severn Valley line;
November Sunday - almost dusk:
lamps at Highley station shine.

Mist is rising on the river,
      you linger by its side:
mysterious now, the waters gleam;
swans in ghostly courses ride.

On the platform people thronging,
      a minute still to pause:
excitement as the train pulls in,
eager rush to carriage doors.

Scarcely seeming like November
      so summer-warm the day:
you roamed in woodland, climbed the hills,
walked through lanes and bridleway.

Red sparks flying past the window,
      you feel the engine's power;
by trees and hedgerows steaming home,
more than twenty miles an hour!

Still you think of field and pathway,
      the Borle Brook running high;
bright bars of sunlight on the bridge;
kestrels swooping down the sky.

Last train back to Kidderminster,
      all Sunday journeys done:
the night grows cold - but memories keep
warmth from this November sun.

E F Scott

THE CHANGING SEASONS

The changing seasons mirror love,
And looking into the mirror above our own assumptions
We catch the mood of each season and match
The possibilities against our own experience,
For whatever the season there is always a sunrise
To embrace the dawn.
Each season an age in itself like love can only trace
The pattern of birth, maturity and death
Before resurrection repeats the story in everlasting glory
Upon the breath of timelessness.
All seasons find flesh in images from the mind,
And the poetry of spring begins from a bare landscape
As if youthful earth is practising for its summer display.
The escape of the first leaf from bud awakes all creation to raise
A hymn of praise on this first spring day for the perfection to come
Where each wild primrose its shape knows is folded in reverence
to the sun.
Too soon the eyes of spring begin to read the story of summer
afternoon,
As adolescent love draws its early sketches from which portraits
emerge,
So spring can only urge the river to flow on
Until a new season is shadowed into being.
Summer day speaks of love born from April showers
And the soft passing winds of May.
The early roses kiss the lips of summertime
And double dreams of love are sewn into a rhyme found on the lips
of lovers.
Autumn mists come and go while age and love sit together
Like a silent leaf folded against a cool breeze
Till winter trees like old age and old love
Smile through the cold air knowing their love will last
Across the changing seasons.

Pat Isiorho

NIGHT GLEANER

4am, grey blend of night with morning,
familiar street, now empty as my bed:
I lean upon the sill, awaiting lamp-set . . .

She comes, sleek gleaner, pacing routine paving
on feet precise and silent as a cat's,
black nose intent, intelligent, alert.

A risky night-moth flutters from warm tarmac:
the vixen snaps, and tidies as she goes,
as she has tidied recent tennis court

of loser's game-set-match dropped biscuit -
which must suffice until the infants' school
and guilty sandwich tucked in privet hedge.

Between her snacks, she pauses, knows my vigil,
turns dark-bright eyes, implying 'Time is brief,
two miles ahead the cubs wait in the lodge.

Tonight I take them nothing but a lesson:
Hunger, the driving force by which all live.
For mere existence, we. What hungers you?'

I cannot tell. From night's ambivalence
I glean, as well as she, by stubborn will,
the sustenance that sees me through the day.

Nora Rock

SEA HORSES

Prancing into formation, fleetingly distant on the horizon,
cavorting and rearing, white-capped flowing manes.
A pulsating posse of gun-metal greys and sleek bays,
proud palominos with glistening pelts, warring battalions.

Mystical and riderless, wide winged wild Olympians
canter in parade marching forward, twenty plus abreast
and over a dozen lines into the hazy distance deep.
Moving out, galloping, surging, flying wave on wave.

They emerge and converge forming a cavalry convoy,
vapour embroiled spumes of thunderous molten hoofs.
A ceaseless scintillating charge, a shore-bound assault,
skimming and scudding nearing the landing stage.

Over the top they surge, wave after wave, engulfing
boulder rock, shingle and dune-topped sandbanks.
Breaching all man-made sea defences, to then disperse
and vanish, reforming once more, on that far, distant horizon.

John Hirst

THE PATH OF MY LIFE

As I walk the path of life I
sometimes stray.

At the moment I am standing on
rough ground, in a forest where the
trees shade the sun.

I know I am just one step
away from my path, my path will
lead me to a gate: behind the gate is a
beautiful field and in that beautiful
field the sun is shining.

It is now decision time! I
could stop where I am or I could
make just one step to my path; all I
have to do then is open the gate.

Why? When all I have to do
is make a simple decision in my life:
do I have to think hard about it first?

A B Harper

To A Dreamer

Dream your dreams my dear,
Be not ashamed, nor ever fear
The scorn of those who never know
The longing in your mind.
Our waking dream is all
We sometimes have to help recall
The kinder moments left behind.

Dreams will help us heal
Our unshown wounds, and oft reveal
Emotions deep, our secret thoughts
And searching heartfelt needs.
Such dreams will ease the way
Through restless hours, doubts of today,
Then sow tomorrow's living seeds.

And so our hopes take root,
Some stay a dream but some bear fruit.
Without that hope life has no warmth,
And love must have its flames.
We need the strength it gives
To keep our faith, to guide our lives,
Fulfil our wants, achieve our aims.

Those who cannot dream
Are without hope - this surely seems
A heartless void, a lonely path.
What is there to atone?
What could the future find?
So dream your dreams, be calm of mind,
For those who dream are not alone.

Catherine Clough

THE DEVIL'S CLAW

In the darkness rain beat down,
Pounding on my weary crown,
I thought about my small cabin,
And all the warmth contained within.
As I walked along the street,
I spied an object near my feet,
As I bent down to examine more,
I noticed it was a devil's claw;
As I grasped it in my hand,
A quiet rumble crossed the land,
The sound became a mighty roar -
A voice called out:
'Your faith no more'
The Devil rose up from the ground,
As lightning cracked and boomed around,
The Devil let a fearsome roar:
'Give me back my other claw'
The Devil sneered,
'I'll take your soul;
'Twill be like all the days of olde,
It shall be as it was before -
But I must have my other claw!'
I dropped the claw onto the floor,
The Devil hissed:
'Your faith no more'
I grasped a lantern from the wall,
I threw it at the Devil tall,
The flames consumed him one and all.
The Devil was no more.

And still when nights,
Are cold and dreary,
And I sit so warm and weary,
I sit and watch my devil's claw,
Which now hangs on my cabin wall,
I hear a voice:
'Your faith no more.'

A W Kennedy

KWAI MEMORIES

Such a modest little span, dull grey,
High above the muddy, swollen waters,
Single glinting track disappearing
Into the jungle's dripping green.
We listen. No barked commands
In Japanese, or squadies' banter,
Only the chatter of crickets,
And the muffled shouts of boatmen
Calling on the river below.
Curious pilgrims with water bottles
And inoculations, we came here
To this place of aching memories
In air-conditioned comfort
From well-starred Bangkok hotels.
In the clammy heat of afternoon,
We walk back across the bridge
To a tranquil village where old men
Sit in shadowed places, remembering.

John C Bird

THE PILOT

Whether I'm flying to Zurich,
New York, Paris, Rome:
I know that you're in charge, Lord,
That we're never on our own.
Yes, we study the controls
And check for safety, that's true!
And welcome passengers on board
With greetings from the crew.
They wear their seat belts,
Watch the films,
Drink whisky, coffee, tea,
With one or two exceptions,
Completely trusting me!
But you're my guiding Pilot, Lord.
I pray to you to guide
Us safely over mountains, seas,
Till the runway is in sight.
And when the wheels have touched down
On some far-distant part,
I always say a 'thank you'
And know deep in my heart
That all the world was made by You.
The more I see, I find
The joy of travelling is a gift
You've offered to mankind.

Marion Payton

CAUGHT IN A DAY

Brightly coloured cushions
Brightly coloured walls,
The whiteness of nets
That waft into halls,

The sunshine that's captured
For this day alone,
Is caught in your breath
That I make my own.

You talk of Romeo
And I of Juliet,
Of Mercutio's demise,
That if we forget

That all life and time
In a bee's drone is found,
The pureness of faith
The smile of a clown,

Then a day like this
Will forever be lost
To an endless winter,
The hardness of frost.

So for now this day
Is all we need,
Make love, and love -
Let this be our creed.

Roy Westwood

DEVIL'S ADVOCATE

I fornicate with Lucifer
And feed the sadist within.
He takes my pure and clean
And leaves my lustful sin.
I feign decency; I'm a cynic
For he manipulates my head.
The inflicted thoughts he provokes
Are symbolic of evil and dread.
I yield for his desire
Take pleasure from mutilation.
Ravenous whispers on rancid breath
Cause my asphyxiation.
I suffer his insatiable needs
To be left bare and tender,
But the emotions he destroys
Allow me to revel in his splendour.
I yearn to be his incarnate
To defile and cause such pains.
But I am feeble and weak
And still blister from his flames.
For the devil has me damned
For I'm still tortured from his spell
And I crave the fetish he gave me
Of our amity gouged in hell.

Hayley Beddoes

ONLY KIDS BELIEVE IN MIRACLES

Only kids believe in miracles,
Their innocent minds not yet exposed to the world
The death, the pain, the suffering,
That comes with the weather
But sticks like the pungent smell of fear.
Their minds stray from the real threat,
The sick taste of an aftermath.
Yet only kids believe in miracles
Their soft wispy hair touched by angels as they sleep.
They have yet to be exposed to the torment that life brings,
The emotional hell that tags along for the fun of it,
Pulling down on your life's esteems.
Only kids believe in miracles.

Suzanne Sephton

REFLECTIONS

In my youth had I known you
When innocence was bliss,
O' joyous rapture now my love,
Could I have captured this.

From a life filled with anguish,
Endured with tainted sorrow,
No more to weep as dawn appears,
Happy to wake the morrow.

Only now has full meaning,
As love and hearts entwine
For now is then and then is now,
One hope, shall thou be mine.

Carol Elizabeth Robinson

DEATH OF A PIER

At Weston by the sea
There used to be a pier,
It held so many memories for me,
Time lapsed had made them very dear.

The pier is now tormented metal
And in its agony of death,
The girders crushed by sea and time
As if about to take last breath.

You cannot walk along her breadth
And step to make wood creak,
Down to the little rock pools
Where a crab or two might sleep.

There is no picnic allowed here
With parents, uncle and aunt,
For they are also gone with time
(Forget them I just can't)

And as I look on dying mass
My eyes are filled with sadness,
How could a pier just crumble away,
To let it must be madness.

In this fickle, rat race time
Things worth saving are oft pushed out,
The pier at Weston is worth saving
And of this fact I'm in no doubt.

Gillian Ackers

AND WE ALL SANG

The birds sang, and space became eternity.
No inhibitions limiting our dreams, until they were reality.
And then repeated into another dream,
Until harmony with ourselves and our universal soul
Moved us, yet we remained unchanged.
For we are all one. One knowing, one being, one One.

We are each our God and each our God is one.
Each star, each galaxy is us. And we are them.
We came from them and they from us, before our time began.
Together we will bloom and birds will sing again,
To signal our return back to the womb
Who knows what then!

Dennis Turner

PRICELESS GIFTS

Sometimes it's good to remember those things in life that are free
Like a colourful summer sunset or spring blossoms on a tree
The birds' resounding chorus as they greet the dawn of day
To stroll the pleasant countryside and see new born lambs at play
Watch the acrobatic swallow as he wings the summer breeze
Take the coastal path at night and hear the symphony of the seas
The colours of the rainbow that follows a summer shower
To explore the world of dreams or breathe the scent of a blooming
flower
Relive again the memories from the pages of our past
The friendship of a partner that's strong and made to last
But along the road of life a priceless asset you will find
Is God's gift of a healthy body and a peaceful state of mind

Patrick Greaves

FINAL WHISPER

Tears sting my eyes when I think of the short farewell I gave you.
Before my return you lay helpless; dying; your eyes large;
your body weary,
Resting in dignified silence, in your special place.
When I entered the room, a wave of emotions washed up within me.
You were not able to see my eyes as I held you,
Nor hear me, as I whispered a secret wish into your ear:
You were waiting to share that moment with me,
And no-one will ever know what we felt at that time.
And though it passed between us in a moment, it could have
been an eternity.
Then silently, in my momentary absence, leaving all your
reminders behind,

You passed on.

Louise Maguire

ON REFLECTION

Looking into the mirror
Tentatively,
Nothing peers out from within its fragile world.
A myriad of invisible shadows,
Nothing mocks my human form,
For its reflection is only that
Of the mind that stands before it.
It is Nothing that pushes me
Further aside and out
Of what is happening
And what is real.
Slowly, I began to lose control
And in the wake of blurred recognition
I begin to see.

Only
Nothing will remain.

Feryad A Hussain

FINAL JOURNEY

At life's end I'm like a ship at sea.
The land recedes and disappears from view.
The mists descend, you can no longer see.
I'm sailing on the gentle seas of blue.
But do not grieve, the other side I see
And family and friends are waiting there.
I'm greeted like a spirit that's set free
With open arms and love of heaven to share.

Marjorie Meath

THE TREE

The sun shone serenely down on the tree,
its leaves soaking up the hot rays which filtered through the clouds
above.
A breeze causes the leaves to rustle gently like confetti spraying down
on a smiling bride.
The bark is cracked, twisted and green,
knolls peer out as if the spirit of the tree was using them as eyes,
to look down on the house which stood basking in its own glamour.

But beneath the boughs of the tree lies a dark, damp, decaying desert,
from which grass pokes up optimistically searching for a small ray of
sunshine to spill through the canopy above.
Chestnuts hang in their spike-studded cases protected until they fall
from shelter into danger below.

I sit beneath its leaves, which provide an umbrella of calm and wonder
what tales this tree could tell.
Would it speak of highwaymen hiding amongst its leaves?
Or would it laugh and tell of young boys climbing up its rough bark,
leaping to the soft ground below?
And would it sigh as it remembered and wish for those times again?
And if it did, would anyone listen,
Or would it just be lost in the bustle of the world below?

Naomi Cochrane

MARCH

My pace was slow
as my feet dragged
through frozen snow
on empty hawk-picked paths.

The day was grey
and muffled by an endless cloud
which hung too low and tight
to let a spark
in contact with the warming sun
ignite.

Helga Hopkinson

TIDE OF DISCOVERY

With trousers rolled above the knee,
He scans the sand now moulded by the tide,
There, ridges show the movement,
Of the constant lapping water,
Where seaweed tangled lies laid bare,
Scallop shells in shades of brown and cream lie buried deep,
As fingers push to flick an upturned shell,
As now within its cavity revealed wet sand,
Pebbles glisten striped and plain,
Scattered as if at random thrown by the unseen hand of the sea,

Sand and shingle pushes now between the toes,
As walking on the shore reveals,
Remnants of a thousand lives once now crushed remains,
Sharp the jagged edges that pierce the sole,
Across the beach litter lies at random dropped,
A polystyrene cup that skips along,
Light and at the mercy of the breeze,
Cigarette ends here and there,
Tilted lie like drunken soldiers on parade,
Until footsteps bury them once more,

The sun glints down upon an aluminium can,
Once with liquid nectar filled now empty cast aside,
Seek the crab within his crevice,
In a rock pool hiding,
First a claw peeps out and then,
One sideways movement gone from view,
Many miles are covered in this quest for a worthy find,
All in a beachcomber's dream,
Tomorrow is another day to while way,
In search amongst the microscopic grains.

Ann G Wallace

LIFE

I have all I want now.
All a girl can ask for,
I'm happy,
Content,
Alive,
My life is slipping slowly into place.

I still have worries
(doesn't everyone?)
I don't know where to go,
What to do,
When to go.

This seems unimportant,
Live life for today,
Not tomorrow,
Life's too short,
I try not to worry.

Enjoy it,
Live it,
Be alive,
Survive,
Just always be happy.

That's what life is about.

Helen Whitmore

ZEN AND THE ART OF MANANA - GROWING

As I slide back my patio doors at morn,
I give my weed-infested lanky lawn
Some dank, half-int'rested consideration.

Standing reluctant, as my coffee cup
Curls steam about my nose to wake me up;
Instead of fragrance I get accusation.

Before me, in the jungling garden's growth,
Unprofitably burgeoning from sloth,
A zillion insect legs in stridulation,

And in the trees, where sunlight paddles free,
The business-crows discuss the price of tea,
And tradesmen-starlings drum up occupation.

Below the privet's greenish gloom, a thrush
Knocks hell out of some snails and pecks the mush,
Thinking that breakfast betters meditation.

This chorus, big with business of the day,
Urges my sleeping mower to make hay
In sun and WD-fortification.

It slyly grins at me through rusting teeth,
Making daft jokes about a blasted heath;
Its wit, like mine, lacks some sophistication.

My neighbour's pigeons 'tsucroo' on the fence,
And 'tut-tut' too, in pigeon insolence,
Praising with faint damns my rustication.

Cutting remarks no mustard cuts with me,
Next time I vote, for Swampy it will be,
And all wild things that tend to relaxation.

Here is one man who will not go to mow,
Declining to reap what nature chose to sow,
All things, say I, in careful moderation.

The forecast's good tomorrow; I will rise
And, with the grasshoppers, I'll exercise
My talent for procrastination.

N R Worrall

SUBMISSIONS INVITED
SOMETHING FOR EVERYONE

POETRY NOW '99 - Any subject,
any style, any time.

WOMENSWORDS '99 - Strictly women,
have your say the female way!

STRONGWORDS '99 - Warning!
Age restriction, must be between 16-24,
opinionated and have strong views.
(Not for the faint-hearted)

All poems no longer than 30 lines.
Always welcome! No fee!
Cash Prizes to be won!

Mark your envelope (eg *Poetry Now*) *'99*
Send to:
Forward Press Ltd
1-2 Wainman Road, Woodston,
Peterborough, PE2 7BU

**OVER £10,000 POETRY PRIZES
TO BE WON!**

Judging will take place in October 1999